"Chase your dream and make your life an adventure."

-Ruben Gonzalez

Ruben Gonzalez
Salt Lake City Olympics

How to Get Where You Want to Be

50 Simple Ways
to Reach Your Goals
Faster than You
Ever Thought Possible

by Four-time Olympian
Ruben Gonzalez

Olympia Press

How to Get Where You Want to Be

by Ruben Gonzalez

ISBN -13: 978-0-578-49894-2

Printed in the United States of America

Published by Olympia Press
Colorado Springs, CO
832-689-8282

Praise from Top Achievers

"If you read Ruben's books or listen to Ruben speak, your life will change for the positive!"

Lou Holtz
Legendary Notre Dame Football Coach
Author of *Winning Every Day*

"Ruben speaks from both his head and his heart, and inspires ordinary people, convincing them they can do extraordinary things. Ruben is persuasive, enthusiastic and very real. Invite him to speak to your group and you'll be glad you did."

Zig Ziglar
Motivational Teacher
Author of *See You at the Top*

"This is one unbelievable success story! Ruben's story is motivating and inspiring!"

Dr. Stephen Covey
Author of *The 7 Habits of Highly Effective People*

"Ruben's story of hard work, dedication and commitment, leading to success in the greatest competition in the world is inspiring and uplifting in a wonderful way!"

Brian Tracy
Author of *Million Dollar Habits*

"Ruben's authentic, he's done it, and he's just like each one of us. You need your team to get Ruben's story of Going for the Gold!"

Denis Waitley
Author of *The Psychology of Winning*

"Ruben will fill your people with the intensity and desire to be their very best. Your company deserves to hear him and his message!"

Tom Hopkins
Author of *Mastering the Art of Selling*

"Ruben is a great speaker. He's real, he's authentic and he lived what he teaches. If you get a chance to have Ruben speak at your event, don't miss it."

Dave Ramsey
Best Selling Author,
Nationally Syndicated Radio Talk Show Host

"Ruben's books are filled with excellent advice. Apply their teachings and watch your life change!"

Ken Blanchard
Author of *The One Minute Manager*

"Ruben has a unique ability to motivate and challenge his audiences. His compelling story provokes us all to set and reach lofty goals!"

Jack Canfield
Author of *The Success Principles*

"Ruben hits you with the absolute truth about what it takes to succeed in the real world."

Jim Rohn
Tony Robbins' Mentor

"Ruben's life confirms an age-old truth; determination, faith, and believing in your God given abilities are still some of the keys to personal success."

Wally Amos
Founder of Famous Amos Cookies

"Ruben will inspire you to pursue your dream, equip you to get through the struggle, and encourage you on to victory!"

Rudy Ruettiger
Inspiration for the movie, *Rudy*

Congratulations

You've just taken a step towards making your dreams a reality. Most people wish about their dreams and talk about their dreams, but they don't act on their dreams. The simple fact that you're investing in yourself by reading this book shows you're doing something to get you closer to your dream.

Zig Ziglar said that you have to "be" before you can "do" and you have to "do" before you can "have." By investing in yourself, you are becoming more capable of reaching your dream. You're stacking the odds in your favor.

This Book Could Change Your Life

(But only if you apply its information)

Following these five tips will help you turn the information in this book into habits that will change your life:

1. **Read this book more than once.** I've read both *"Think and Grow Rich"* and *"The Magic of Thinking Big"* every year for the last 20 years. The more times you read a book, the more you become like the book.

2. **Underline and make notes.** Make sure you have a pen and highlighter in hand. Underlining specific lines and paragraphs will triple your retention rate. Write your own thoughts in the margins and own this book.

3. **Re-read your underlines.** Re-read your key items over and over. Record and listen to your notes.

4. **Apply the material immediately.** Doing so will help you understand the material better. Don't try to be perfect. Done is better than perfect.

5. **Prioritize what you want to learn.** Select one to three things from the book, apply them faithfully and make them a habit.

This book is dedicated to my parents, who taught me the values and principles that helped me realize my dreams.

Contents

Part 1

The Success Principles
52 Key Principles Top Achievers Use to Win

Part 2

How to Make This Your Best Year Ever
Over 100 Tips to Help You Develop a Winning Mindset so You can Realize Your Goals Faster

Part 3

You Can Do It!
Ruben's Most Popular Forbes Articles

How to Win the Gold Medal in Your Own Life

How to Get Yourself to Boldly Pursue Your Goals

How to Get Started on the Way to Your Dream

How to Keep Small Thinkers from Stealing Your Dream

How to Create Momentum and Reach Your Goals

The Courage to Succeed

When I was 10 years old, I was watching the 1972 Sapporo Winter Olympics on TV and I knew right away that I wanted to be an Olympian. I was drawn to the Olympic athletes. What drew me to them wasn't their athleticism, it was their spirit.

The Olympians were a group of people that were willing to fight for their dream for many years with no guarantees of success. From that day on I read everything I could about the Olympics. I could tell you everything about the Olympics but I was afraid of taking action because I was never a great athlete. In fact, in PE at school, I was always the last kid they picked to play sports.

Several years went by. I remember being glued to the TV whenever the Olympics were on. In 1980, when the US Miracle Hockey Team beat the Russians at the Lake Placid Olympics, my belief started growing. I was inspired, but my fear still kept me from taking action.

Finally, in 1984 I saw Scott Hamilton win the Gold Medal in figure skating. When I saw Scott win, I said to myself, "If that little guy can do it, so can I. I'll be in the next Olympics. It's a done deal. I just have to find a sport." Watching Scott Hamilton's performance lit a fire in me. I was finally ready to take action.

I was 21 years old. Way too old to learn a new sport, but when the dream is big enough, the facts don't count.

I had no time to lose. The next Olympics were only four years away and I had to find a sport. I went to the library to do some research. When I looked at a list of the Summer Olympic Sports I said to myself, "You have to be a super athlete to do any of these things. There's no way." Then I took a list of the Winter Olympic sports. I realized I needed to find a sport that fit my strengths. My strength wasn't athleticism. My strength was perseverance. In fact my nickname in High School was "Bulldog." So I thought, "I have to find a sport that's so tough, a sport with so many broken bones in it, that there'll be a lot of quitters. Only I won't quit. I'll make it to the top through the attrition rate."

I had it down to three sports. Ski jump, bobsled, and luge. I lived in Houston, Texas. Hot, humid, sticky Houston. I'd never skied before so forget ski jump. That would have been suicide. And bobsled? Where was I going to find three other people in Houston that would want to do the bobsled? That left the luge. I'd never even seen the luge on TV before. If I had, I doubt I would have done it. It's crazy. All I had was a picture of a guy on a luge. I said to myself, "That's the sport for me." That's how I picked my sport.

I didn't even know where the luge track was. So I wrote Sports Illustrated and asked them, "Where do you go to learn how to do the luge?" They wrote back saying the track was in Lake Placid. I called the Luge Association in Lake Placid and got myself into a beginners program. Just a couple of months after watching Scott Hamilton win the Gold in the Sarajevo Olympics I was in Lake Placid learning how to luge.

They put me in a class with fifteen other brand new sliders. It was brutal. The toughest thing I've ever done. Every day fewer people would show up for practice. Bt the end of the first season I was the only one left from that group. The first two years I was crashing four out of five times. But I kept at it. After a while I was crashing only one out of five times. Then one out of ten. By the end of the second year I was crashing only one out of a hundred. I finally figured out how to drive that crazy sled.

Over the first few years I broke my foot twice, my knee, my elbow, my hand, my thumb, and a couple of ribs. My attitude was that a broken bone was just a temporary inconvenience because bones heal. On the third season I started competing internationally to try to qualify for the 1988 Calgary Olympics. On the fourth year I made it. I got to compete in four Olympics by the skin of my teeth. Four Olympics each in a different decade. As I jokingly tell my audiences, "It doesn't mean I'm good. It just means I'm old!"

Marching in the Opening Ceremonies is the highlight of the Olympics. You don't march into the stadium. You float in. For two weeks you walk around with a silly smile on your face. It's Heaven. It really is. Competing in the Olympics was worth every sacrifice. It was worth getting hurt. It was worth driving a beat up old car. It was worth maxing out my credit cards and getting into huge debt. It was worth the years of hard training and the bitter cold.

I'm a better person for having put myself through the struggle. I'm stronger, more confident, and I've learned things about myself that will help me for the rest of my life.

What were the chances that someone like me would make it to the Olympics? One in a million? One in ten million? I probably had a better chance to win the lottery!

I was just an ordinary kid with an extraordinary dream. I wasn't a big shot. I was a little shot that kept on shooting. Just like that young, scrappy U.S. Hockey Team that beat the mighty Russians. Just like Scott Hamilton. That's all they did. They believed in themselves and they just kept on shooting.

And that's something you can do too. If you start believing in yourself, you give it all you've got, and you refuse to quit, it'll be just a matter of time before you make your dream come true, too; and just a matter of time before you start creating a better life.

Success is a choice. It's your choice. Make a decision that you'll face your fears and that you'll do whatever it takes to get started. Make the decision to get off the stands and into the arena. Make the decision to stop existing and to start living.

What's your Olympics? What's your dream? If you'll dedicate your life to the pursuit of your dream, you'll be making your life a masterpiece. You'll live a rich life and you'll be an inspiration to everyone around you.

Part One

The Success Principles
52 Key Principles Top Achievers Use to Win

"Make Your Life an Adventure!"

- Ruben Gonzalez

1 Decide to Become a High Achiever

Pursue your dream. Make your life a masterpiece by being willing to pay the price of success. Achievers know that in order to realize their dreams, there's a price to be paid. They're willing to sacrifice, struggle and work hard with no guarantees of success.

"Success is to be measured not so much by the position that one has reached in life as by the obstacles which he has overcome while trying to succeed."

- Booker T. Washington

Can you think of a time when you had to dig deep and work hard to reach a big goal? How did you feel when you reached it?

2 Take Advantage of Anything That Will Help You Reach Your Goal

Successful people are constantly looking for anything they can use to gain an advantage. They look ahead in order to position themselves to be in the best place when opportunity strikes. Think ahead. By thinking ahead and planning ahead, you'll have an advantage over the competition.

"The time to repair the roof
is when the sun is shining."

- John F. Kennedy

Can you think of a time when you were able to take advantage of an opportunity by thinking ahead and positioning yourself to win?

3 Your Attitude Determines Your Altitude

Your attitude is simply your frame of mind. It's how you see things. It's whether you focus on the possibilities or on the challenges. Positive thinking doesn't guarantee success. But with positive thinking, you're a lot more likely to succeed.

"Things turn out the best for the people who make the best out of the way things turn out."

- John Wooden

Think of a time when you were going through a challenge but you decided to "protect your attitude" and remain positive. How did it go for you?

4 Make the Law of Averages Work for You

The more you fail, the greater the chance that you'll ultimately succeed. You can actually fail yourself to success. Because every time you fail, you gain experience. In my case, I crashed my way to the top. For two years I crashed on four out of every five luge runs. But I learned something from every crash. Then, on my third year, all of my luge knowledge came together, and I hardly ever crashed anymore.

"I am not discouraged, because every wrong attempt discarded is another step forward."

- Thomas Edison

Think of a time that you persevered even when continuing seemed crazy. What happened? What did you learn?

5 Believe in Yourself and Believe in Your Dream

If you believe something is possible, and your attitude is that you're willing to do whatever it takes for as long as it takes to get the job done, then success is just a matter of time. You can increase your self belief by the books you read, the audios you listen to, and the people you associate with. If you put good things in your mind, you will become stronger and you'll believe more in yourself.

"Whether you think you can or you think you can't, you're right."

- Henry Ford

What are three books that would help you reach your goals?
Who are three people you could call or meet
that have done what you would like to accomplish?

6 Use Your Power to Choose

No matter what your circumstances, you have the power to choose how you'll react. You have the power to choose who you'll associate with, what you'll do with your free time, what books you'll read, and what action you'll take in the next five minutes to get you closer to your goal. Your dreams are there for the taking. Will you create a magnificent life? It's your choice.

"Everything can be taken away from a man but one thing; the power to choose one's attitude, to choose one's own way."

- Viktor Frankl

What's something you could do today to help you reach your goal?

7 Think Empowering Thoughts

What you think determines what you do. What you consistently think about will determine where you'll end up. That's the reason why associating with like-minded winners is so important. By creating a dream team and regularly associating with them, you'll set yourself up to succeed by peer pressure.

> "What's going on in the inside shows up on the outside."
>
> - Earl Nightingale

Who are five successful people you could meet with on a weekly or biweekly basis? Call them up and set up a mastermind group.

8 Believe That Everything That Happens to You is for a Reason

Learn to look for the silver lining behind every cloud. There are powerful lessons to be learned from every challenge. Challenges are there to slow us down long enough for us to learn lessons we need to learn on the road to our dreams.

"I always turn every disaster into an opportunity."

- John Rockefeller

What have you learned from your latest challenge?

9 Focus All Your Efforts

Figure out what's most important to you and focus all your efforts accomplishing it. When you focus all your efforts on one goal, your chances of success are almost guaranteed. If you split your focus between two goals, your chances of success drop to 66%. If you have three goals, your chances of success are only 25%. Top achievers focus on one goal. After achieving it, they move on to the next goal.

"The number one rule of success is the ability to apply your physical and mental energy to one problem incessantly without growing weary."

- Thomas Edison

What goal will you focus 100% of your effort on?

10 How to Become Self-Confident

Confidence comes from preparation. Confidence doesn't come from "faking it until you make it." Confidence comes from practicing a skill until you master it. Once you master a skill, you become confident. Once you master your field, you'll become confident. With confidence, you can start accomplishing things you never imagined.

"Confidence doesn't come out of nowhere. It's the result of hours and weeks and years of constant work and dedication."

- Roger Staubach

What skills do you need to master to reach your goal? Decide to practice those skills until you master them.

11

Nip Negative Thoughts in the Bud

The biggest challenge on the way to success is mastering ourselves. No matter what you're doing, you'll always have times when you doubt yourself, or times when you have inner conflicts and desires that make you want to do things that will keep you from your goals. Constantly ask yourself, "What's the next thing that I can do right now to get me closer to my goals?"

> "He who overcomes his desires is braver than him who conquers his enemies; for the hardest victory is the victory over self."
>
> - Aristotle

What's the next thing that you can do right now to get you closer to your goals? Find an accountability partner that will make sure you get it done.

12 Take Control of Your Own Life

You control all your decisions. Whenever you give control to someone else, you cease to be master of your own fate. Whenever you take personal responsibility for your actions, you maintain control. Take responsibility and you'll hold the tiller of your life's ship. If it is to be it is up to you.

"If you don't run your own life, someone else will."

- John Atkinson

Think of a time when you took responsibility for a bad result or a mistake. How did it make you feel to own up to your actions?

13 Work Through Other People

Developing people skills is important because you can accomplish a lot more with other people than you can ever accomplish by your own efforts. Get good at showing others how they can truly benefit by teaming up with you. Learn leadership skills so you can enlist people to help you accomplish your mission in life.

"Coming together is a beginning; staying together is a progress; working together is success."

- Henry Ford

Who are three people you could team up with in order to reach your goals faster?

14 Develop the Courage to Succeed

Courage means becoming bigger than your circumstances. Courage isn't the absence of fear. It's acting in spite of your fear. To succeed in life you need two types of courage. The courage to take action and the courage to endure. The courage to take action comes from believing in yourself. The courage to endure comes from your desire to succeed.

"Expect trouble as part of life and when it comes, hold your head high, look it squarely in the eye, and say, "I will be bigger than you. You cannot defeat me."

- Ann Landers

Think of a time when you faced your fear.
Didn't you feel great afterwards?
Did you realize that the fear was a smokescreen?

15 Win One Step at a Time

There's no such thing as an overnight success. You have to lay the groundwork day by day for a long, long time. You must win many private victories before you experience a public victory. Football games are won one play at a time. Businesses are built one customer at a time. Every accomplishment is the result of many smaller accomplishments.

"Do not despise the bottom rungs
in the ascent to greatness."

- Publilius Syrus

Can you think of an example of a big project you finished that took a lot of small steps? Graduating from school, training for a marathon, losing weight, etc. Think about how every step is important in order to reach the final goal.

16 Learn from Your Mistakes and Position Yourself to Win

Opportunities come and go. Life has cycles that come and go like the ocean's tides. When a surfer misses a wave, they don't waste precious energy by getting upset. They learn from their mistake, make an adjustment, and position themselves to take advantage of the next wave. Become an opportunity surfer. Put yourself in a position to win.

> "Luck is the sense to recognize an opportunity and the ability to take advantage of it."
>
> - Samuel Goldwyn

Think about a time when you made a mistake, and immediately made an adjustment to position yourself to win.

17 How Badly Do You Want Your Dream?

How badly you want something will determine if you'll get it. If you want something badly enough, nothing will make you quit and you'll figure out a way. Desire gives you the power to pay the price of success. You can develop desire, fuel desire, and sustain desire by vividly imagining your desired outcome, correctly using affirmations, and by associating with like-minded people.

> "Nothing can resist a will which will stake even existence upon its fulfillment."
>
> - Benjamin Disraeli

Is there something you want so badly that you lose sleep thinking about it? What are you doing every day to fuel your desire so you will take the action to eventually get it?

18 Do Something You Enjoy

Find an arena you are suited to work in. Do something you enjoy. Do something that you would do for free. Life is too short to do anything else. If you love your work, you can't help but be successful.

> ## "I never did a day's work in my life. It was all fun."
>
> ### - Thomas Edison

What do you love the most about your work?
If you hate your job you need to quit and do something
you'll enjoy. That'll free up your position
for someone who'd love to do what you do.

19 How to Double Your Income

Take the average of what the five people you spend the most time with make in a year, and you'll get your annual income. Ninety percent of success is determined by who you hang around with. Why? Because successful people think differently than unsuccessful people and you become like the people you associate with. If you want to double your income, start hanging around people who make twice what you do.

"You are the product of your environment. So choose the environment that will best develop you toward your objective."

- W. Clement Stone

Make a list of five people you need to be spending time with. Five people who are already getting the results you'd like to be getting.

20   Go for the Gold

Top achievers are not content with mediocrity. They don't settle for second best. They're not satisfied to simply do things just like others have done them. Winners always want to raise the standards. They want to excel and want everything they do to be of first class quality. They go the extra mile. They put uncommon effort into common tasks. Focus on doing everything with excellence, and you'll build a reputation that will take you to the top.

"The kind of people I look for are the eager beavers. The guys who try to do more than they are expected to."

- Lee Iacocca

Are you excited about your work?
What are some ways you could add
excellence to your work?

21   **Expect the Best**

Whenever you believe something is possible and you act accordingly, the world conspires to make your dreams, plans and aspirations a reality. Sooner or later, those who win are those who think they can.

> ## "If you paint in your mind a picture of bright and happy expectations, you put yourself into a condition conducive to your goal."
>
> ### - Norman Vincent Peale

Think about what it's going to feel like when you realize your dream. Get your senses, your feelings and your passion involved. Paint an emotional picture in your mind and your subconscious mind will figure out a way to reach it.

22 Double Your Failure Rate and You Will Double Your Successes

Successful people accept failure as part of life and decide to make the most of their failures. They see every setback as a lesson to be applied in their journey towards success. They understand that failure is simply part of the process and that avoiding temporary failure guarantees permanent failure.

"Failure is only the opportunity to more intelligently begin again."

- Henry Ford

Think about a recent failure and try to find the lesson. Make a plan on how to use that lesson to reach your goal.

23 If You Have Hope in the Future You Have Power Today

Hope sees the invisible and accomplishes the impossible. Napoleon said that a leader's number one job is to give his people hope. Because when people have hope, they'll fight for their dreams. When they lose hope, they quit. Surround yourself with encouraging people - people that will instill hope and faith in you so you can be all you were created to be.

"Faith is to believe what we do not see. The reward of faith is to see what we believe."

Saint Augustine

Make a list of the most encouraging people you know. List three ways you can instill hope in your people.

24   Act in Spite of Your Fear

If you hesitate in the face of fear, the fear will grow. If you boldly do what you fear, the fear will disappear. Because fear is simply a state of mind. It's just a smokescreen. Don't let fear control you. Destroy fear with bold action. Courage is acting in spite of your fear. Cowardice is running from your fear. Which do you want to be? Courageous or cowardly? It's your choice.

"You gain strength, courage, and confidence every time you look fear in the face."

- Eleanor Roosevelt

Think about a time when you felt fear but took action anyway. Maybe when you jumped from the high dive as a child. How did it make you feel?

25 You Have to Sow Before You Reap

You have to plant the seeds before you can reap the harvest. The more you sow the more you'll reap. If you plant a kernel of wheat, you'll reap a pint. If you plant a pint, you'll reap a bushel. You always reap more than you sow. Don't judge each day by the harvest you reap, but by the seeds you plant.

"The man who will use his skill and constructive imagination to see how much he can give for a dollar, instead of how little he can give for a dollar, is bound to succeed."

- Henry Ford

How are you sowing for the future right now?
Making sales calls, building relationships
with possible prospects, reading the right books?

26 Always Set Goals

The purpose of goals is to focus our attention and give us direction. The mind will not look for answers until it has a clear direction. When you have a crystal-clear goal, magic happens. You start receiving ideas and thoughts that lead you to your goal. Life without goals is boring. Life with goals is an adventure. Write your goals first thing every morning. It's an act of commitment that sets the stage for a productive day.

> "The world has the habit of making room for the man whose words and actions show that he knows where he is going."
>
> - Napoleon Hill

Are you writing your goals down every morning?
Do you regularly think about what it will feel like
when you reach your goal?

27 Commit to Personal Development

The most successful people in every field are constant learners. They regularly read books, listen to audio programs and attend seminars. They understand the "slight edge" rule. If they learn and apply a new idea that gives them a slight edge, they can beat the competition. Invest in yourself, and as you grow as a person, you'll leave your competition behind.

"You are what you are and where you are because of what's gone into your mind. You can change what you are and where you are by changing what goes into your mind"

- Zig Ziglar

Are you regularly reading personal development books and books about your industry?

28 Your Habits Will Make or Break You

Your habits will lead you to failure or success. That's why associating with winners and reading the right books is so important. Because you become like the people you associate with. You pick up their habits. And the habits determine the outcomes.

> "The books you read and the people you meet will determine where you are in five years."
>
> - Charlie "Tremendous" Jones

Are you regularly meeting with key people that can help you become more successful? If not, who are three people you could be meeting with? Call them up and start meeting with them.

29 How to be Happy

You can't pursue happiness. Happiness is a byproduct of three things; the quality of your relationships, the degree of control you feel you have in your life, and using your gifts and potential in the pursuit of a worthy goal or dream.

If you want to be happier, work on improving your relationships with the most important people in your life, and chase your dream with all your heart and soul.

"Satisfaction lies in the effort, not in the attainment. Full effort is full victory."

- Gandhi

Who are the most important people in your life?
What are you doing to strengthen
your relationship with them?

30 Honesty Pays Huge Dividends

Short sighted people don't understand that every action has consequences. Good deeds are rewarded and evil deeds are punished. It's better to fail with honor than to succeed by fraud.

"To measure a man, measure his heart."

- Malcolm Forbes

Think of a time when by doing the right thing,
even though it cost you in the short term,
you were able to gain in the long term.

31 Success is a Decision

Your life is a series of decisions that you make based on the choices you have at that moment. Whenever you are deciding between two choices, ask yourself, "Will this choice get me closer to my goal?" If the answer is yes, then make the decision and take immediate action on your choice.

"Life is the sum of your choices."

- Albert Camus

Are you laser focused on reaching your goal? When faced with a decision, do you consider how it will impact your reaching your goal?

32 Bounce Back from Your Challenges

People on skid row have something in common. They all had a major challenge that made them quit on life and they are eager to tell you all about the situation that conquered them. They are constantly feeding their fear.

Successful people react differently when they get knocked down. They bounce back up, learn their lesson, forget the situation that knocked them down, move forward, and leave the past in the past.

> "It's not what happens to you.
> It's how you handle it."
>
> - Ruben Gonzalez

*Do you like to wallow in your misery
or do you look for the lesson in every setback?*

33 Become a Person of Action

1. Focus on what you can do now.
2. Don't wait until conditions are perfect.
   Done is better than perfect.
3. Ideas by themselves are useless.
   Ideas acted upon are priceless.
4. If you act and face your fear, the fear will disappear.
5. Don't wait until you feel like doing something. Taking immediate action will create the feeling to take even more action.
6. Don't waste time getting ready to do something. Start now.

"Anyone can do nothing."

- Ruben Gonzalez

What can you do in the next 10 minutes that will get you closer to your goal?

34 You Will Become What You Think You Are

You get the kind of treatment you think you deserve because others see in you what you see in yourself. If you think you're inferior, you'll act inferior and others will treat you that way. How you think determines how you act and how you act determines how others will react to you. The more respect you have for yourself, the more respect others will have for you.

"Change your thoughts and you'll change your world."

- Norman Vincent Peale

How do you see yourself?
How do you conduct yourself
in front of other people?

35   How to Build Confidence

1. Think only positive thoughts.
2. Replace negative thoughts with positive thoughts.
3. Walk faster. Walk with purpose.
4. Stand in a confident manner: head up, shoulders back, stomach in.
5. Look people in the eye and smile.
6. Introduce yourself to others. Don't wait for them to introduce themselves to you.
7. Speak your mind.

"Face your fears head on."

- Ruben Gonzalez

Do you look people in the eye?
Do you introduce yourself to other people?
Do you speak your mind?

36

Don't Make Excuses

Successful people don't make excuses. They could, but they don't. An excuse is an alibi that helps someone save face when they aren't producing the results they should be producing. Nobody wants to hear your excuses. They just want to know that you intend to do what you need to do to get the results you are after.

"Excuses are a waste of time. Successful people don't waste time. They use their time to look for ways to become more successful."

- Ruben Gonzalez

When things go wrong do you take responsibility or do you make excuses?

37 Belief Gives You the Power to Take Action

Belief is the first step to success. Once you believe, you can start working on figuring out "how" you'll accomplish your goal. Wishful thinking has no power. The "how will I do it" always comes from belief. When you believe, you'll attract helpers because all of a sudden they'll start having confidence in you. Belief determines what you'll accomplish in life.

The best way to increase your belief is by reading good books and associating with successful people.

"Man is literally what he thinks."

- James Allen

Are you reading good books
and associating with successful people?

38 Fall in Love with the Process

"When I was 15, I had a clear vision of myself winning the Mr. Universe contest and was driven by that thought. I had such faith in the path, that it was never a question in my mind that I would make it."

Driven by his vision of becoming Mr. Universe, he worked out five hours a day, loving every minute of it, because he felt that each time he went to the gym, he was one step closer to winning the competition. At the age of 20, Arnold Schwarzenegger became the youngest man to win the Mr. Universe title.

> "Trust the process, fall in love with the process, and work the process to win."
>
> - Ruben Gonzalez

Do you think of your work as the vehicle to your goals and dreams? If you do, you'll work harder and you'll enjoy it because your work will have purpose.

39 Take Advantage of Opportunities

Opportunities are like waves. You have to start paddling to catch the wave or else you lose. Winners don't hesitate. They take advantage of opportunities.

"There is a tide in the affairs of men, which, taken at the flood, leads on to fortune; omitted, all the voyage of their life is bound in shallows and in miseries... and we must take the current when it serves, or lose our ventures."

- William Shakespeare, Julius Caesar

Do you take immediate advantage of your opportunities?

40 Choose the Right Arena for You

You'll be successful once you find an arena you're suited to play in. Most people spend their whole lives in the wrong arena. By chance, they've chained themselves to bad jobs, bad relationships, or bad association. If this describes you, then you need to break free. You need to break those chains that hold you back and start playing in an arena designed for you.

> "The test of a vocation is the love for the drudgery it involves."
>
> - Logan Pearsall Smith

Is your job a good fit for you?
Does it require you to use your strengths and your gifts?

41 Partner up with Key People to Reach Your Dreams

Don't ever let the lack of know-how or lack of resources keep you from pursuing your dream. When you lack know-how or resources, look for key people you can partner up with. People who have the skills and resources you need to move forward.

"Teamwork makes the dream work."

- Ruben Gonzalez

Who are 3 people you can start meeting with who will help you reach your goals?

42 Protect Your Attitude

Studies of successful people show that attitude accounts for 80% of their success and aptitude for only 20%.

What is attitude? Thinking like a winner. Expecting to win. Being willing to pay the price. Deciding to make it happen. Believing you can do it. Positive expectancy. Confidence coupled with a strong work ethic.

"What happens to you is less significant than what happens within you."

- Louis Mann

Do you protect your attitude?
What things do you say to yourself
when things don't go your way?

43 Start Making More Decisions

Leaders make decisions all the time. Followers make suggestions. Making suggestions is easy because it requires no action or risk of failure. Making decisions is tough. It takes guts because there's always something at stake.

Start making more decisions. Start taking more action. The more you do, the more of a leader you'll be, and the more you'll advance both personally and professionally.

"Great decision making comes from trusting and following your intuition and your gut feelings."

- Ruben Gonzalez

Do you trust your intuition? Do you trust your gut feelings enough to regularly make decisions?

44 Persistence Pays Off in the Long Run

At the age of 21 he failed in business.
At the age of 22 he lost a race for State Legislature.
At the age of 23 he failed at his second business.
At the age of 25 his girlfriend died.
At the age of 26 he suffered a nervous breakdown.
At the age of 28 he lost a race for Congress.
At the age of 30 he lost another race.
At the age of 33 he lost yet another race.
At the age of 38 he lost a race for Congress.
At the age of 45 he was defeated for Vice President.
At the age of 49 he was defeated for Senate.

At the age of 50 he was elected
President of the United States.

A life riddled with failure helped make Abraham Lincoln tough enough to be able to lead the United States through the Civil War. If you're going through struggles in life, you're being prepared for a big important purpose.

"Character is forged whenever we struggle."

- Ruben Gonzalez

Think of a season in your life that was filled with struggles.
What did you learn from your struggles?
Did you use that knowledge to succeed afterwards?

45 Quick Tips for Success

1. Don't fear the competition.
   Respect your competition.
2. The harder you work,
   the better prepared you'll be.
3. Pay attention to details.
4. Know yourself. Use your strengths.
5. Hustle and effort will
   make up for your mistakes.
6. Be true to yourself. Follow your heart.

"Success is no accident. It's hard work, perseverance, learning, studying, sacrifice and most of all, love of what you are doing or learning to do."

- Pelé

*What small but important things
are you doing every day to reach your goals?*

46 Don't Second Guess Yourself

It's easy to look back and see where you might have done something differently. As long as you're looking for ways to improve your performance, it's OK to look back. But don't waste time second-guessing yourself. Your past results were based on your past experience. If things don't work out, use your new experience to get better results next time.

> "Your attitude is too precious to hurt by second-guessing yourself. Protect your attitude because it's the key to your future success"

> \- Ruben Gonzalez

Do you look for the lesson in every failure or do you second guess yourself when failing?

47

Prepare in Order to Win

Set your sights on a goal but focus on preparation - on what you must do and think to accomplish your goal. Winning is a by-product of your preparation and effort. Focus on the effort and preparation and your results will take care of themselves.

"Failing to prepare is preparing to fail."

- Vince Lombardi

Are you preparing to win?
What books could you be reading that will prepare you
to win more? What three people with the expertise
and resources you need could you be meeting with?

48 Always Play Full Out

Total effort is what counts. As long as you do your best, there's no shame. Whether in your job, in the community, or in your personal life, always do your best. You can't control being better than someone else. But you can control doing everything to be the best *you* can be. Personal success comes from total effort. If you do less than your best you have failed yourself.

"Peace of mind comes from knowing you did your best."

- John Wooden

Are you giving it your all to reach your goal?
What is one more thing you could do today to win?

49 Redefine Failure

If you know in your heart that you did the best of which you were capable, there's no such thing as failure. That's why full effort is so important. You always win when you make the full effort. It's not about the dream. It's about the person you become in the pursuit of the dream.

"In great attempts, it is glorious even to fail."

- Wilfred Peterson

Are you doing everything you can possibly do to reach your goal? Who could you call today who could help you reach your goal? Call them.

50 Take Massive Action

You have what it takes to win big in life. You just need to take action. Massive action. That's what successful people do. They figure out where they want to be and then they jump into the arena and take action. Along the way they constantly develop themselves to become even better at what they do. By using the ideas in this book you'll be on your way. You can do it. Don't wait. Start now.

> ## "You miss 100% of all the shots you don't take."
>
> ### - Michael Jordan

What's your dream?
Are you ready to take action
and make your life an adventure?

51 Ruben's Rules for Success

You'll never achieve anything great in life until you start believing that something inside of you is bigger than the circumstances you face.

You can become great by making a decision to pursue your dream in life and by refusing to quit.

Every success you've ever had or will ever have is the product of your courage to act and the courage to endure.

Success isn't about how much talent you have. It's about what you do with the talent you do have.

Successful people love the battle, the challenge and the journey. It's about knowing that you did your best.

If you do whatever it takes for however long it takes, success is only a matter of time.

52 The Champion's Creed

I am a Champion.
I believe in myself.
I have the will to win.
I set high goals for myself.
I have courage. I never give up.
I surround myself with winners.
I'm cool, positive, and confident.
I'm willing to pay the price of success.
I love the struggle and the competition.
I stay relaxed and in control at all times.
I focus all my energy on the job at hand.
I vividly imagine what victory will feel like.
I am a Champion and I <u>will</u> win.

For a free full color 8x10 printable version
of "The Champion's Creed" visit:
TheChampionsCreed.com

"Far better it is to dare
great things, to win glorious
triumphs, even though
checkered by failure, than to
rank with those poor spirits
who neither enjoy much nor
suffer much, because they live
in the gray twilight that knows
neither victory nor defeat."

- Theodore Roosevelt

Part Two

How to Make This Your Best Year Ever

How to Reach Your Goals Faster by Developing a Winning Mindset

"The difference between a successful person and others is not a lack of strength, not a lack of knowledge, but rather a lack of will."

- Vince Lombardi

How to Make This Your Best Year Ever

Count your blessings daily.
Doing so will keep you in a positive state of mind.

Surround yourself with positive, encouraging,
successful people. They'll pull you up
no matter what the circumstances.

Come to terms with the fact that in life
there's no free lunch. Pay your dues.

It's not what happens to you,
it's how you handle it.

Deliver more than you're paid to.
Make yourself indispensable to others.

Focus on your strengths. Find an arena
you're suited to play in, have the courage
to get started, have the courage to not quit,
and decide you'll give it all you've got
for as long as it takes to get the job done.

Don't let others rain on your parade.
Avoid negative people like the plague.

Decide to find the seed of good in every adversity.

Decide that you are willing to do
whatever it takes to realize your dream.

Realize that true happiness lies within you.
Happiness is the product of the quality of your
relationships and of the degree of control
you feel you have in life.
Every time you make excuses,
you lose control and become unhappy.

The past doesn't determine the future.
No matter how many times you have failed,
the next time you could succeed. If you don't believe it,
just read Thomas Edison's biography.

Protect your attitude.
Your attitude determines your altitude.
Average talent with great attitude will beat out
great talent with bad attitude every time.

Live this day as if it were your last.
Treat others as if it were *their* last day.

Take your projects seriously
but learn to laugh at yourself.

Don't neglect the details. Excellence comes
from taking care of the details.

Smile more. It makes you more approachable,
and makes it easier to build your dream team.

Constantly ask yourself, "What is the number
one thing I could do in the next 15 minutes
to get me closer to my goal?"
Then do it right away.

Break down large goals into smaller
more manageable goals.

Find a mentor who believes in you,
who'll support you, and who'll
push you toward your dream.

Whenever in doubt, go with the bolder choice.
Base your plan on your strengths.

Humble yourself to the leadership of those
who have done what you want to do.
Ask for help and you'll succeed faster.

Believe in yourself.
Persist in the face of challenges.
Don't take "No" for an answer.

Celebrate every small victory.

Follow your heart.

Constantly look for ways to simplify your life.

Anger gives people courage to do things
they usually wouldn't do. Whenever you're angry,
don't waste your anger doing negative things.
Harness the energy in your anger to reach your goal.

Take advantage of change.
Change brings another opportunity to win.

Read biographies then model your life
after the lives of successful people.

Don't complain about your circumstances.
Decide you'll make your own circumstances.

Don't kid yourself. Life is hard.
Success takes time and massive action.

You only live once. Go for the Gold.
Decide you won't simply exist.
Decide to live an exciting life.
Don't just take up space. Make a difference
so you'll be missed when you're gone.
Decide to leave a legacy.

Be willing to pay the price of success.
No pain no gain.

Vividly imagine what your victory will feel like.
Replay that victory all the time.
It's your preview of coming attractions.

Act in spite of your fear. No guts no glory.

Watch less TV.
Your TV is keeping you from your dreams.
TV is the electronic income reducer.

Establish a mission and a purpose for your life.

Burning desire creates the power to succeed.
Develop a passionate desire for your purpose.
How badly you want it to happen will determine
if you do make it happen.

Never blame, whine or complain.

Talk positively to yourself.
Never bad-mouth or criticize yourself.

Be a good finder. Look for good in everything
that happens. Developing a positive mental attitude is a
decision. A decision that helps you create a better life.

Fly with eagles, and you'll start to think,
feel and act like an eagle.
Hang around with turkeys, and…
well, you get the picture.

Know when to listen and know when to speak.

If you're not failing you're playing too safe
and you're not growing. If you want
to succeed faster, double your failure rate.

Bite off more than you can chew.

Live your life with passion.

Become a lifelong learner.
Read good books, listen to self-development audios,
and attend seminars.

Forgive others quickly. Being angry
at someone else is like drinking poison.

Make your dream so exciting
that it takes your breath away.

Every time you make an excuse you give away
control of your life. Stop making excuses.

Do what you fear and the fear will disappear.

If you want to win big
you have to be willing to lose big.

Focus on your goals, not on your obstacles.

You'll only see it when you believe it.

Don't let other people's opinion of you
become your reality.

When your "why" is big enough,
the "how" will take care of itself.

If you're not excited about your dream,
don't expect others to get excited about your dream.

Don't listen to the naysayers in your life.
"Impossible" is just the opinion of somebody
who doesn't believe as much as you do.

Write your dreams in concrete and your plans in sand.

Write down your goals by hand every day
before you turn on your computer.
It takes less than a minute and helps you
start off the day in a more purposeful, focused manner.
Doing this will make you more productive
than 95% of people in the world.

Imitate the perseverance of the people you admire.

Read 15-30 minutes a day from
a positive self-development book.

Become a part of a support group.
Hang out with people who have
goals and dreams similar to yours.

Know yourself. Know your strengths and weaknesses.
That knowledge will help you understand why you act
the way you do. Learn about the four personality types.

Help others reach their dreams.

See challenges as an opportunity
to become stronger.

Set high goals for yourself. If you're not
headed anywhere in life, you're headed nowhere.

Wanting to win is not enough.
You have to be willing to prepare to win.

Take more chances. You'll never know
what you were missing in life
until you dare to pursue your dream.

Insanity is doing the same thing and
expecting different results. To get better results
you must constantly adjust your approach.

Fortune favors the brave. Boldness has magic in it.
Don't play it safe. Start taking more chances.

Winners have the courage to get started
and the courage to endure.

Do the things you fear
or else fear will control your life.

Having long term goals makes it easier
to make good short term decisions.

When somebody laughs or makes fun of you,
that person should stop having any influence in your life.
They are holding you back from your purpose in life.

Whenever somebody compliments you,
they've just seen a glimpse of your greatness.
The compliments you get over and over
are a clue to where your gifts lie.
When you use your God-given gifts to realize
your dream, you make the world a better place.

Associate with big thinkers.
Big people don't laugh at big ideas.

Success is all about guts and vision.
Knowing what you want,
and having the guts to go after it.

As long as you don't quit, you've still got a chance.

You'll either pay the price of success
or the price of regret.
The price of success weighs ounces.
The price of regret weighs tons.
It's your choice.

People of integrity expect to be believed,
and they're willing to let time prove them right.
The easiest way to keep your word
is to under promise and over deliver.

It's human nature to be lazy – to want to coast.
Therefore, constantly strive to improve, because he who
stops being better eventually stops being good.

You're not finished when you are defeated.
You are only finished when you quit.

The greatest predictor of future success is how
driven and passionate you are to realize your dream.
Passion is much more important than talent.

Have fun. You can't get passionate about anything
if you aren't having fun. If you aren't having fun
you're probably doing the wrong thing.

Take a leap of faith. Leap and the net will appear.

Take full responsibility for your results.

Commitment creates opportunity.
Stop talking and start doing.
Think less and act more.

The day you take complete responsibility
for yourself, the day you stop making excuses,
is the day you start moving to the top.

Believe that there's an opportunity in every challenge.
Your job is to find it and to take advantage of it.

If it is to be it is up to you.
Nobody can succeed for you.
You have to make it happen.
There's no one to stop you but yourself.
Success is a decision.
Decide you'll make it happen.

Fear is a smokescreen. Act in spite of your fear
and the fear will disappear.

Invest in yourself. The better you are,
the better your results will be.

Control your thoughts and you control your life.

Create a crystal-clear picture
of what you want to accomplish.

Serve others. Your rewards in life
will be proportionate to the value
of your service to others.

Think about the future instead of the past.
Focus on what you can do today
to improve your future.

Discipline yourself to focus on the solutions,
not on the problems.

Find out what other successful people
in your field are doing, and do the same
things yourself over and over.

Whatever you think about all the time
will grow in your life.

"Work smart, not hard" is a joke.
If you want to succeed, you'd better work smart and hard.
The harder you work, the luckier you'll be.

Believe that you're the master of your own destiny
and that you can create your own future.

Focus on doing things that will improve your odds
of winning. It's all about improving your odds.

All your actions have consequences.
If you sow massively, you'll reap massively.

There are more opportunities today
than there have ever been.
Take advantage of them.

If you have an intense desire to achieve something,
it's a given that you have the ability within you.
Your job is to figure out how.

Always expect the best.
We tend to get what we expect.

Be willing to try different approaches on the way
to your goals. When a football team doesn't
score a touchdown, they don't move the goalposts,
they change the play.

Winners understand that the road to success
is filled with failures and challenges.
Winners fail their way to success knowing that
one big success will cancel out all the failures.

Assume that success is only a matter of time.
Resolve to learn something from every setback,
and decide that quitting is not an option.

Your persistence will fuel your self-belief
and your self-belief will fuel your persistence.
But you have to decide that quitting is not an option.

Positive self image doesn't come from people
praising you. Confidence and positive self image
come from competence. They come from being good
at whatever you do. And that comes from practice.
Confidence and positive self image come from
constantly facing your fears and refusing to quit.

Everything you do is either getting you closer
or further from your dream. Everything.

Don't live life through others.
Be the hero in your own life.

When opportunities appear, move quickly.
Doors of opportunity close as quickly as they open.

You can't do anything about the past,
therefore, remove the words "I should have…"
from your vocabulary. "Should haves," create guilt,
suck the wind out of your sails, and drain away
positive energy that you could use to
do something about your problem today.

Constantly ask yourself, "What can I do right now to
reach my goal?" Then, do it right away.

When you move boldly in the direction of your dreams,
unseen forces will come to your aid.

What would you dare to do
if you knew you could not fail?
What are you waiting for? Do it now.

Act as if it were impossible to fail. Everyone's afraid.
Courage isn't the absence of fear.
Courage is acting in spite of your fears.
Face your fears and conquer them with swift action.

Limiting what you are willing to do
limits what you will achieve.

The books you read and the people
you associate with will determine
where you are in five years.

You determine your habits.
Your habits determine your future.

Nothing of value comes without effort.
Decide you'll do whatever it takes.
Decide you are willing to pay the price.

The secret of your future
is hidden in your daily routine.

High achievers have a drive
that most of us can't even begin to imagine.
They work every day at catching their breaks.
They're ordinary people with extraordinary drive
and work ethic. You can develop the same drive.

Success is a decision. It's all up to you.

Successful people always talk about
and think about what they want to happen.
Unsuccessful people always talk about and
think about what they don't want to happen.
You attract what you talk about.
What are you talking about?

Make no small plans. Small plans and dreams
don't have the power to inspire and motivate you.
Have a dream that takes your breath away.
Only such a dream will motivate you to take action.

Start seeing things and people
as they can be, not as they are.

Winners are willing to do the things
losers aren't willing to do.

Think big. Focus on the possibilities,
not on the problems.

The faster you stop operating
from a state of wishful thinking and
get passionately committed to your dream,
the better your life will be.

When you achieve your dream, pursue another dream.
That's how to live a life of adventure.

Understand this about the steepness of the slope as you
approach the summit of any competition. Be it luge in the
Olympics, basketball in the NBA, or being the most
successful business in your field, there's as much
difference between number 10 in the world
and number 5 as there is between number 100 and
number 10. Going from number 5 to 4 is the same like
going from 10 to 5. And from 3 on up it is inconceivable.
What that means is that whenever you plateau at
any level and you want to get to the next level,
you'd better be willing to put forth much more effort.

Don't let other people's weaknesses
get in the way of your strengths
and rob you of your dream.

A dream gives you energy, hope,
and keeps you from wasting your life.

If you have no critics,
you likely have no successes.

Once a year, read "How to Win Friends and Influence People," "The Magic of Thinking Big," and "The Power of Positive Thinking."

Every morning, get in front of the bathroom mirror, and serious as a heart attack, tell yourself what your dreams and goals are. Repeat this every time you are in front of a mirror. Do this and in time you'll become unstoppable.

Develop people and leadership skills. The only way to accomplish great goals is by building a team and working through other people.

What you believe will determine what you will do. What you do determines your results. Change your beliefs, and you'll change your results.

When you work hard enough and long enough that you start believing that you deserve to succeed, you'll start acting like a deserving person and success will come to you.

Show up for practice.
Champions show up for practice.

People who make excuses have no direction in life.
No dream. They don't know where they're going.

Go from one failure to another without losing enthusiasm.
Go from one success to another without losing humility.

Mental toughness – Have fun, focus on the task
at hand, be passionate, bounce back from failures.

Every time you do something you fear,
every time you step up and look fear in the face,
you gain strength, confidence, courage, and faith.

The struggle, the sacrifice (giving up something good
today for something better tomorrow) of doing the right
thing ennobles you. Behaviors do not just serve our
physical needs, they serve our spiritual needs as well.

You don't have to justify your actions.

Success is a decision. You decide to do
whatever it takes for as long as it takes to make it.

Your ability to succeed is in direct proportion
to your ability to take rejection.

Levels of commitment – I'll try, I'll do my best,
I'll do whatever it takes, it's a done deal.

Big people don't laugh at big ideas.

The only thing in life
which does not require effort is failure.

Learn to love the struggle.

Double your failure rate. Failure is the best teacher.
Success lies just on the other side of failure.

Find a dream big enough to overcome your fears.

Plant with bold faith and stay around for the harvest.

Keep your eye on the target
and look for different ways to reach it.

If you talk about it, it's a dream,
if you plan it, it's possible,
when you take action, it's real
and it starts to change your life.

Set people up to win. Especially in the beginning.
In the beginning, people's actions are very limited
because they think they have limited potential
(they can't see themselves far into the future).
If you have limited belief, you're going to use limited
potential, and you're going to take limited action.
That's why you break goals down into manageable tasks,
to keep your belief level high.

You can't win if you're not in the game.

There's dignity in being willing to fight.
Dignity in being willing to take the journey.

You have a noble purpose in life.
Figure out what it is and dedicate your life to it.

The reward for doing right is mostly internal;
self-respect, dignity, integrity, and self-esteem.
Doing right gives you a sense of order,
calm, and peace. You sleep better.

Seize the day, accept responsibility for the future,
chase your dream, never quit,
and people will say you're lucky.

The 95% rule says – There's a 95% chance
that 95% of everything you know about
life and business and success has come from people
in the bottom 95% group. If that is true (and it is),
then how do you expect to get top 5% results?
That's why you need to hang around the top 5% group.

The will that weakens first strengthens the other.
If you back down from something you fear,
the fear for that thing gets stronger.
If you boldly face your fear, you get stronger.

Don't assume anything.
Get the specific information.
Assuming sets you up to be a fool later.

Don't worry about what others think about you.
What matters is knowing who you are
and believing the possibilities for your life.

Focus on the possibilities
and take control of your own destiny.

Don't waste your anger. Whenever you get mad,
learn to channel that anger in a positive way.
Passion is positive anger. All progress comes
from people who are mad and dissatisfied.
They are sick and tired of being sick and tired.

We're not living in the agricultural age or
in the industrial age. We're living in the information age.
The people armed with the best information and willing
to apply it will win. That's why the people you associate
with and the books you read will determine your destiny.
Are you reading the books that will help you realize your
dreams? Are you associating with the people who will
help you realize your dreams? If you're not, you're
fooling yourself.

The more you persist in the face of adversity,
the more you like and respect yourself.

Your support team is a constant source
of power and strength.

Protect and nourish your dream.
Protect your attitude. That's the basis of success.

A movie without a challenge to overcome
and a destination to reach is boring.
The same is true about a life with
no goals or challenges to overcome.
In order for life to be an adventure
there must be a goal.

Being great means being misunderstood.
Don't ever fear being misunderstood.

Take full responsibility of the job you do.
It is a reflection of you.

Face your fears and do it anyway.

The size of a person's bank account
is proportional to the size of a person's library.
Poor people have big TVs and no books.
Rich people have small TVs and huge libraries.
They're too busy applying what they learn
to have time to watch TV.

Most people feel trapped in their circumstances.
They don't realize they have the power to change.
Fear holds them back. Face your fears.

There is a part of us that wants to have
passion, hope, optimism and energy.
The part that is sick of having to put up
with the roles assigned by the world.
The part that doesn't want to be controlled.
The part of us that is genuine,
yet the part of us that usually lives in silence.

Most people are not living the life they want
or the life that they would choose.
Most people live a life that pleases other people
but not themselves. Their hearts are not in it.
It is not natural. So everything is a chore.
There is no passion, no excitement.
That's why you need to dedicate your life
to the pursuit of your dream.

People ignore their real dreams.
Being someone you're not
is the hardest thing you will ever do.

Most people don't allow themselves
to be themselves. And by doing that,
they cheat themselves and they cheat everyone else.
And yet since it feels safe, they persist in living life
with that dull ache inside.

If it doesn't come from your heart
it's not really you. And it won't be fun.
So take that leap of faith and go for it.
If you jump the net will appear.

If you will embrace and consistently and
persistently apply these principles,
you'll amaze people with all you accomplish.
People will say you are lucky,
but you'll know luck had nothing to do with it.

Chase your dream. Never Quit.

Part Three

You Can Do It!

"You gain strength, courage and confidence every time you look fear in the face. The danger lies in refusing to face the fear, in not daring to come to grips with it. You must make yourself succeed every time. You must do the thing you think you cannot do."

- Eleanor Roosevelt

How to Win the Gold Medal in Your Own Life

The principles I used to make it to the Olympics will help you reach your professional and personal goals.

The following tips will help you develop the mental toughness and attitude of champions.

Don't Worry About what Others Think

What other people think is completely subjective because it's based on where they are in life. Some people will think your performance is stellar and others won't be impressed. Just focus on your goals and on your daily actions. Athletes are advised not to read their press clippings. Why? Because you don't want your attitude to be affected by other people's opinions.

It's OK to Make Mistakes

If you're not making mistakes you're playing it too safe and you're not trying hard enough. Average people don't make a lot of mistakes. Look at mistakes as learning opportunities. At the beginning of the luge season we slide on sharp steels. Sharp steels have a lot of traction but they're slow. As the season progresses, we gradually round our steels in order to slide faster. We trade traction for speed. When we start crashing we back off a bit.

Be willing to take risks so you can see what your true limits are.

Perform for Yourself, Not to Impress Others

As soon as you take your eyes away from your "why," the core reason that drives you to do what you do, you'll lose the "eye of the tiger," your passion and your motivation. Keep your "why" fresh in your mind and don't try to impress others.

Focus on What You Can Control

The only things you and I can control are our thoughts and our actions. I can control how hard I train, what I eat, who I associate with, what I read, etc. I can't control what my competition does. On race day if I know I did everything I could to prepare, I can feel proud of myself regardless of the results.

Don't worry about your competition or the economy. Focus on what you can do in the next 15 minutes to move your business forward.

Don't Get Hung by the Tongue

Watch your self-talk. Keep it positive. Don't bad mouth yourself or others. What you say determines what you think. What you think determines what you do. What you do repeatedly becomes your habits and your habits determine your results. It all starts with what you say to yourself.

Take Responsibility for Your Performance

The luge is the only Olympic sport timed to the 1/1000th of a second. We take four runs and the athlete with the lowest total time wins. If we have a slow time we can't blame the judges or the wind or anything else. It's all about how we prepared our sled and how we drove the course.

If you're not getting the results you want, talk to your mentor and make an adjustment so you can improve your performance next time.

Aim for Improvement, not Perfection

Perfectionists seldom accomplish much because they wait for everything to be perfect before they even get started. Conditions will never be perfect. You just have to start.

Get started and get some coaching from someone who's already done what you want to do. Get feedback. Then take more action. And so on. By alternating action with feedback you'll constantly improve and the results will take care of themselves.

Celebrate Your Successes

Take time to celebrate the small successes on the way to reaching your big goals. Celebrating lets your subconscious mind know that you did well and refuels you emotionally for the next push. Have fun. Ask yourself, what would be a fun way to do this?

The more fun you have, the better you'll perform because you'll be looser, less stressed, and more likely to get in the zone.

Stay in the Moment

Put on the blinders and focus only on what you're doing right now. When at work focus on work. When you're at home focus on your family. At the beginning of a luge run, when I'm doing a luge start I focus on one thing at a time. When I'm pulling from the start handles I focus on the pull. When I'm paddling, I focus on the paddles. When I'm settling down on the sled from sitting down to lying down, I focus on the settle. And then I focus 100% on the section of the curve that I'm sliding on. That's the only way I have a chance of doing my best down the whole run.

Focus on what you are doing right now and you'll perform to your highest potential.

Focus on the Journey and the Destination

Focus on the journey to enjoy the road to success and focus on your "why" and your destination so you stay on course. Looking back, I see that getting to compete in four Winter Olympics was incredible, but my favorite moments were the good times our team mates had when traveling from track to track. The friendships I made and the person I became were the byproducts of pursuing the Olympic dream.

Follow these simple tips and you'll win the Gold Medal at work and in life.

How to Get Yourself to Boldly Pursue Your Goals

Why do people play it safe? Why do they hesitate instead of boldly attacking their goals and living life to the max? Because fear gets the best of them.

Most people let fear of the unknown and fear of failure keep them from pursuing their dreams. Fear is a thief. If you let it, fear will rob you of your goals, your dreams and what could be the best of your life.

Most people picture the worst case scenario. They visualize the worst thing that could possibly happen and then the fear immobilizes them.

But think of it this way -- no one should fear failure, because when you fail to get the results you want, all you need to do is try a different approach. The only time fear of failure is justified is the last time you're willing to try.

What about fear of the unknown? Fear of the unknown is often just a smokescreen because, if you face your fear, the fear will disappear.

But how do you get yourself to face your fear and act boldly? One way is to reduce the fear by managing your risks.

Whether you're partaking in a risky recreational activity, you have a high-risk job or you're trying to reduce your business risk, there are several ways you can manage your risk. You can't ever eliminate risk, but you can definitely manage it so you'll feel confident about taking bold action towards your goals.

Plan Ahead And Create Contingency Plans

I've been competing in the luge on and off since 1986 -- hurling myself down an icy chute at more than 90 miles per hour while experiencing up to 6 G-forces on the tightest curves.

Most people think lugers are thrill seekers. We're not. The thrill seekers don't make it past the first season. Lugers are analytical. So are many test pilots, race car drivers and mountain climbers. Lugers treat the tracks with respect, and we do everything we can to prepare and to plan our luge runs.

No matter how many times we've been to any track, before taking any runs we walk the track with our coach and come up with a game plan. What lines will we take? How will we steer down the run in order to have the best time?

Then we talk about "escape routes." What will you do if you are too early into curve one? What about if you are too late into curve one? What if you hit the left wall before curve one? What if you hit the right wall? And so on -- for all 15 or 16 curves of the track.

By doing that, we gain confidence because we know we can handle anything the track can throw at us.

The application in business is to rehearse your sales calls and presentations and have an answer for every objection your prospect could possibly have.

Follow A Coach, Guide Or Mentor

Ever since I was a kid, I wanted to climb Mount Kilimanjaro, the highest mountain in Africa. There was something romantic and exotic about Kilimanjaro that drew me to it.

Kilimanjaro is a mile higher than any mountain in the Rocky Mountains. At the peak, the air is much thinner, meaning only half of the oxygen molecules are available for a single breath compared to at sea level. Although it's not a technical climb, every year a few climbers die while trying to climb it.

So, how does a flatlander from Houston climb it? Simple. I hired one of the world's top mountain guides, Dean Cardinale. Dean has climbed Mt. Everest and had climbed Kilimanjaro over a hundred times.

At the trailhead, Dean got really serious and said: "For the next five days, you step wherever I step. You rest whenever I rest. You drink water whenever I drink water. You eat whenever I eat. Most importantly, tell me right away if you feel any discomfort. Because things get worse really quickly at high altitudes. If you follow my lead, in five days you'll get to take a picture on the top of Africa."

Dean taught us how to force oxygen into our lungs by pursing our lips when we exhaled. He taught us the "rest step," which is a special way of stepping that conserves energy. It turns out that climbing a mountain is all about energy management.

I'm not a mountain climber. I'm a mountain follower. By following my guide, I got to climb Kilimanjaro, one of the Seven Summits.

Don't reinvent the wheel. Find someone who's already done what you want to do and follow their advice.

Do Your Due Diligence

Ever since I read Hemingway's *The Sun Also Rises*, I've wanted to run with the bulls in Pamplona, Spain. But unlike most people, I didn't just go do it. Before going to Spain, I read three books about Pamplona and I even called the author of one of the books - a man who had run with the bulls every year for 20 years.

I told him, "I need some tips. I want the Pamplona experience, but I don't want any holes in my body."

He gave me a handful of simple tips that reduced my risk considerably. He told me where to stand, where not to stand, what to do if I fell, to watch out for the drunks because they're more unpredictable than the bulls, to watch out for bulls that have broken away from the pack and a few other nuggets.

By following his advice, I ran with the bulls twice and lived to tell about it.

Don't be rash in the pursuit of your goals. Do your due diligence, get the facts and then you'll be able to boldly take action based on a solid plan.

If you create contingency plans, follow a mentor and do your due diligence, you'll drastically reduce your risk and be likely to take more action and reach your goals faster than you ever thought possible.

"What's easy to do is also easy not to do."

- Jeff Olson

How To Get Started On The Way to Your Dream

One day in February of 1972, I turned on the TV and I saw something that changed my life: the Sapporo Winter Olympics. After watching the pageantry of the Opening Ceremonies and the thrilling competitions, I turned to my younger brother Marcelo and said, "I'm going to be in the Olympics!"

It takes two types of courage to realize your goals and dreams: the courage to get started and the courage to not quit. The courage to get started comes from your belief. If you believe something is possible, you'll get started. If your desire is strong enough, you'll commit to doing whatever it takes to reach your goal. Nothing will make you quit.

When I got excited about the Olympics, I was a 10-year-old with a lot of desire but not an ounce of belief that I could actually do it. After all, in school I was always the last kid picked to play sports in gym class. I was even on the bench when they played kickball.

So, I didn't do anything. I talked the talk but I didn't walk the walk. My dad knew that I liked to read, so he encouraged me to read biographies of great people. He told me that if I did, I'd discover how I could succeed as well.

Reading biographies led to reading personal development books like *How to Win Friends and Influence People, The Magic of Thinking Big, The Power of Positive Thinking,* and countless more. Slowly but surely, I started learning the principles of success and growing as a person.

My dad also encouraged me to associate with successful people so I would pick up their habits and start thinking like them. He said that once I started thinking and acting like successful people, I'd be on the way to my own success.

Over a period of time, I started believing more in myself. I started facing my fears and taking more risks. I started becoming a person of action and I became tenacious and perseverant. Kids in high school started calling me "bulldog."

I was a completely different person from the 10-year-old kid who had a pipe dream of competing in the Olympics. And then, I saw something that drove me to action.

In 1984, while watching the Sarajevo Winter Olympics, I saw Scott Hamilton win the gold medal in figure skating. I said to myself, "If that little guy can win a gold medal, I can be in the Olympics." For the first time, I believed. I knew that I knew that I could do it. I was finally ready to take action. I went to Lake Placid, New York, and took up the sport of luge. Four years and a few broken bones later, I was competing in the Calgary Olympics.

What about you? What's your dream in life? What's in your heart, in your spirit, in your soul? There's a purpose for your life. Are you going after it?

If you're not pursuing your dreams, you're not living — you're just existing.

Henry David Thoreau said, "The mass of men lead lives of quiet desperation." He was talking about the people who are afraid to pursue their dreams.

Those years when I didn't do anything to pursue my dream were hard. I was stagnant, bored and miserable. I was stressed, unfulfilled and angry. I didn't like myself. I was living a life of quiet desperation. I had potential but no drive, no purpose and definitely no courage to face my fears and take action.

Once I started taking action everything changed. All of a sudden, my life had purpose. I had joy in my life because I was working toward something that was important to me. I went from existing to living. All I had to do was start taking action. If fear of failure or fear of the unknown is holding you back, do what I did.

• Start reading personal development books, success principles books, self-help books and biographies.

• Start associating with people who are making things happen - successful people. Find someone who's already done what you want to do and ask them to be your mentor.

• Whatever you do, don't focus on what you don't want to happen. Focus on how great it'll be when you finally realize your dream. Whatever you focus on will get bigger in your life. Focus on what you want.

• Finally, get mad, get passionate and get busy taking massive action. Before long, you'll become known for your dream, you'll attract helpers and eventually, you'll realize that dream. The process of pursuing your dream will help you grow into the type of person who can reach that dream and it'll make you hungry for your next dream. It's all about the person you become.

Don't become known as a person with a lot of potential. People with a lot of potential don't do anything special with their lives. They waste their God-given gifts and talents and regret it later. Be known for your purpose, your drive and your passion for your dream.

Do that and you'll live a joyous life as you make a huge impact in the world.

How to Keep Small Thinkers from Stealing Your Dream

Success is simple but it's not easy.

One of the hardest parts of doing something special, great, or unique, like building a business or creating a new product is putting up with all the naysayers, those people whose only goal in life is to stomp on other people's dreams.

When I was 21 years old I was a bench-warmer on my college soccer team. I had a lot of heart, but I was not very athletically gifted. In fact, I rarely played more than five minutes a game.

Inspired by watching figure skater Scott Hamilton win the Gold Medal at the Sarajevo Olympics, I decided I would take up the sport of luge and set a goal to compete in the Calgary Olympics.

By the way, I lived in hot and humid Houston, not exactly the Winter Sports capital of the World.

As soon as I started telling people about my goal, I was shocked at how many people laughed at me. Some said I was too old, others that I wasn't athletic enough and others still that I didn't even live close to any of the luge tracks.

Very few people encouraged or supported me.

It didn't take long to figure out that there are two types of people in the world - those who are on your team and those who are not.

I made a decision to only hang around the people who believed in me. I couldn't afford to let the critics erode my self-belief.

By associating with positive like-minded people, I was able to stay mentally strong no matter what challenges I faced.

Dreamers and Non-Dreamers

A dreamer will never be understood by a non-dreamer. So don't waste your precious energy trying to make your critics understand you. It'll never happen.

Rob Siltanen, who wrote the copy for the famous 1997 Apple commercial said it best.

"Here's to the crazy ones. The misfits. The rebels. The troublemakers. The round pegs in the square holes. The ones who see things differently. They're not fond of rules. And they have no respect for the status quo. You can quote them, disagree with them, glorify or vilify them. About the only thing you can't do is ignore them. Because they change things. They push the human race forward. And while some may see them as the crazy ones, we see genius. Because the people who are crazy enough to think they can change the world, are the ones who do."

The commercial featured Albert Einstein, Bob Dylan, Martin Luther King, Richard Branson, John Lennon, Thomas Edison, Muhammad Ali, Gandhi, Amelia Earhart, and Pablo Picasso - a pretty good group of people to aspire to be like.

Reasonable people adapt themselves to the world. Unreasonable people persist in trying to adapt the world to themselves. Therefore, all progress depends on unreasonable people.

How You Look to Average People

Imagine you're in a field that's covered with high grass. There's a large hunting dog running left and right, back and forth, barking like mad. You think he's lost his mind. But the dog has a goal, a dream, a purpose. He's chasing a rabbit. That's why he's darting back and forth. Only you don't see the rabbit because of the high grass. To average people you look like the dog. They think you're crazy because they see you but they can't see your dream.

Stick to Your Guns

Don't listen to the critics. Don't let average people talk you from pursuing your purpose. Dis-associate from the nay-sayers and associate with other big thinkers like you. Find those like-minded people that will encourage you and help you reach your goals.

Stick to your guns. Follow your heart. Pursue your dream, and change the world.

"A good plan violently executed now, is better than a perfect plan next week."

- General George Patton

How to Create Momentum and Reach Your Goals

Have you ever gotten excited about the idea of doing something or creating something? Maybe starting a business, writing a book or even doing something really wild, like biking across the United States to raise money for a special cause?

Did you do it? Did you follow through on that urge? Or did you get all practical and realistic and quit before you even got started?

Dreams are very fragile things. When you're inspired by the possibility of an idea, unless you take immediate action, your dream will die and you'll regret it forever.

If you overthink or over-plan something, inertia sets in and you never get started. You talk yourself out of taking action.

The key to making great things happen is to start before you're ready. To take immediate action. To think less and act more. You only have to be courageous for about 10 seconds to do something you fear. After that you're committed and it's easy to keep going.

Just get started. Do something. Don't worry about making mistakes. Making mistakes means you're doing something. That's a good thing. There's always time later to analyze and make corrections. For now, just get going.

Get started right away. If you hesitate for even a second, your mind will start making excuses, justifications, and come up with countless reasons why you can't or shouldn't do what you know you need to do.

If you have the chutzpah, the courage, the "cojones" to take action right away, even before you "think" you're ready, your boldness creates immediate momentum. And then, great things will start to happen.

W.H Murray, the author of "The Scottish Himalayan Expedition," said:

"Until one is committed, there is a hesitancy, the chance to draw back, always ineffectiveness. Concerning all acts of initiative, there is one elementary truth, the ignorance of which kills countless ideas and splendid plans: that the moment one definitely commits oneself, then Providence moves too. A whole stream of events issues from the decision, raising in one's favor all manner of unforeseen incidents and meeting and material assistance which no man could have dreamed would have come his way. I have learned a deep respect for one of Goethe's couplets: 'Whatever you can do or dream you can, begin it. Boldness has genius, power and magic in it.' Begin it now."

When Murray wrote that, he was talking about how the simple act of booking a ticket on a ship to India committed him to follow through and be a part of the Scottish Himalayan expedition. That small act of commitment led him in a direction that changed his whole life.

Buying that ticket was relatively easy to do. But what's easy to do is also easy not to do.

I've taken that approach all my life and it has worked miracles for me. Even though I'm a common man and I'm not particularly gifted in any way, by boldly taking action whenever I was inspired to do something and by persevering when the going got tough, I was able to do some pretty uncommon things.

From Benchwarmer to Olympian

In February 1984, inspired by watching the Sarajevo Olympics on TV I decided I would compete in the next Olympics. I had no right to think that. I was 21 years old and had never been a great athlete. But I took action.

Within three months I was in Lake Placid, NY where I started learning the sport of luge.

I never focused on the probability that I would make it. I only focused on the fact that making it was possible.

Incredibly, four years and a few broken bones later I was competing in the 1988 Calgary Winter Olympics.

From Copier Salesman to Keynote Speaker

Right after the 2002 Salt Lake City Olympics I was asked to speak at a school. After my talk the principal told me I had a gift and I needed to speak for a living. I was a copier salesman at the time.

I'd always wanted to own my own business and the principal's enthusiasm filled me with belief in myself. Three days after speaking at the school I quit my job. I thought, "If I can sell a copier, I can sell a Ruben too."

I built my business by cold calling every school in Houston. Today it's 99% corporate. Over the years I got to share the stage with Zig Ziglar in huge arenas over 20 times. None of that would have happened if I hadn't taken bold action.

Oldest Winter Olympian

After a seven year break and at the age of 55 I started competing again. I'm training for Beijing 2022 where I hope to become the oldest Winter Olympian ever - 59 years old.

My coaches say I have a shot. That's all I ask for. A chance, an opportunity. And that's all you can ask for because there are no guarantees in life. You have a dream, you boldly go for it, you give it all you've got and let the chips fall where they may.

So how about you? What will you do the next time you get excited about the possibility of doing something? Are you going to over-analyze it and ask all your friends for their opinion until they fill you with doubt and make you quit before you even get started?

Or are you just going to go for it? Go for it even before you're ready. That's what people who get things done do. They take immediate bold action. They run to daylight just like top NFL running backs do.

Get off your rear end and do something. Think less and act more. Done is better than perfect. Just throw mud on the wall. Some of it will stick. You can always clean up the mess later. Do something. Jump and the net will appear.

If you'll just do that, you'll be amazed at what you accomplish in your life.

"Whatever you believe you can do, begin it. Action has magic, power and grace in it."

- Goethe

If I Could Do It, You Can Do It

I hope that by now you realize that there's nothing special about me. I'm just a guy who had a burning desire and was willing to do whatever it took, for as long as it took, to make it happen.

I just consistently and persistently followed success principles. Do yourself a favor: don't just read these principles. Apply them. Knowledge is not power. Applied knowledge is power.

I'm proof that these principles will work for anyone. After all, what are the chances that someone like me would go to the Olympics four times? I was just an average athlete, I didn't take up my sport until the age of twenty-one, and to top it off, while living in hot and humid Houston, I picked a winter sport.

I was just an ordinary kid with an extraordinary dream. I wasn't a big shot. I was a little shot that kept on shooting.

And that's something *you* can do too. If you start believing in yourself, you give it all you've got, and you refuse to quit, it will be just a matter of time before you make your dream come true, too; and just a matter of time before you start creating a better life.

About Ruben Gonzalez

A seemingly "ordinary guy," Ruben wasn't a gifted athlete. He didn't take up the sport of luge until he was 21. Against all odds, four years and a few broken bones later, he was competing in the Calgary Winter Olympics. At the age of 47 he was racing against 20-year-olds at the Vancouver Olympics. His story takes people's excuses away.

Ruben's an outstanding storyteller with an incredible story that inspires audiences to think differently, live life with passion, and to push beyond self-imposed limitations and to produce Olympic-caliber results.

Ruben's appeared nationally on ABC, CBS, NBC, CNN, and FOX. He's been featured in Time Magazine, Success Magazine, The New York Times, Forbes, as well as publications all over the world. Ruben's the author of the critically acclaimed book, "The Courage to Succeed."

Ruben speaks from both Olympic and business experience. Before becoming a professional speaker, Ruben was a top producing copier salesman in Houston, Texas. Ruben's client list reads like a Who's Who of Corporate America. He's spoken for audiences around the world; Europe, Africa, Asia, North and South America.

Ruben's presentation is an Olympic experience his audiences never forget. See for yourself, watch his demo video on his website. You'll like it so much, you'll want your whole family to watch it.

Ruben lives in Colorado. He enjoys the challenge of climbing Colorado's fourteen-thousand-foot peaks, snowboarding, sailing and flying powered paragliders.

Inspire Your People to Achieve Olympic Caliber Results

"Phenomenal"
New York Life

"A Home Run"
Kaiser Permanente

"Outstanding"
Microsoft

"Superb"
ConocoPhillips

"Amazing"
Bacardi

Book Ruben to speak at your next meeting or event. To check availability call 832-689-8282

Success Resources from Ruben

Ruben's Monthly Success Tips

RubenTips.com

Ruben's Online Success University

RubenU.com

Leadership and Adventure Retreats

OlympiaAdventures.com

"Success is like wrestling a gorilla. You don't quit when you're tired. You quit when the gorilla is tired."

- Robert Strauss

"Most people want to change the world but don't want to change themselves."

- Leo Tolstoy

"The real competitor wants to do everything better than everyone around him.

He wants to beat everyone. That's the deepest need in his nature.

It has made him what he is. Without it, we would never have heard of him."

- Stirling Moss
Legendary Grand Prix Driver

"I never did anything by accident nor did any of my inventions come by accident."

- Thomas Edison

"The credit belongs to the man who is
actually in the arena; whose face is
marred by dust and sweat and blood;
who strives valiantly; who errs
and comes short again and again;
who knows the great enthusiasms,
the great devotions, and spends himself
in a worthy cause; who at best knows in
the end the triumph of high achievement;
and who at the worst, if he fails,
at least fails while daring greatly."

- Theodore Roosevelt

"If you're going through hell, keep going."

- General George Patton

Make it an Olympic day!

- Ruben Gonzalez